FOLLOW THE LEADER STORIES

Run, Elijah!

CAROLYN NYSTROM

Illustrated by Sharon Dahl

MOODY PRESS
CHICAGO

j222.53
NYS

Carolyn Nystrom is well known as the author of Moody Press's long-lived doctrinal series, Children's Bible Basics. She has written 64 books—some available in ten languages—as well as stories and curriculum material. A former elementary school teacher, she also served on the curriculum committee of her local school board.

Carolyn and her husband, Roger, live in St. Charles, Illinois, a Chicago suburb. As foster parents, they have cared for seven children in addition to their own two daughters. In her spare time, Carolyn enjoys hiking, classical music, gardening, aerobics, and making quilts.

Now award-winning artist Sharon Dahl has teamed up with Carolyn Nystrom to provide lively, captivating illustrations for the Follow the Leader Series. Sharon lives with her husband Gordon and daughters Samantha and Sydney in Boonton Township, New Jersey.

©1998 by
CAROLYN NYSTROM

PD RV AD

All rights reserved. No part of this book may be reproduced in any form without permission in writing from the publisher, except in the case of brief quotations embodied in critical articles or reviews.

Moody Press, a ministry of the Moody Bible Institute, is designed for education, evangelization, and edification. If we may assist you in knowing more about Christ and the Christian life, please write us without obligation: Moody Press, c/o MLM, Chicago, IL 60610.

ISBN: 0-8024-2205-5

1 3 5 7 9 10 8 6 4 2

Printed in the United States of America

"It's never going to rain again," I shouted,
my hands stretched out against a deep blue sky
laced with white fleecy clouds.
"Not until I say so.
King Ahab, this is a message from God."

Then I ran.
And as I ran, those fleecy clouds flittered away—
as if God chased them far from the edge of the earth.

I ran and ran for days and days.
Finally I came to a deep ravine
with high dark walls,
a slit of blue at the top,
and down below a laughing, bubbling brook
named Kerith.

I hid
from those who did not wish to hear
my words from God.

But God was near.
Each day and night His ravens came,
all silky black,
and brought me food.
And Kerith gave me drink.

BRUMBACK LIBRARY
VAN WERT, OHIO

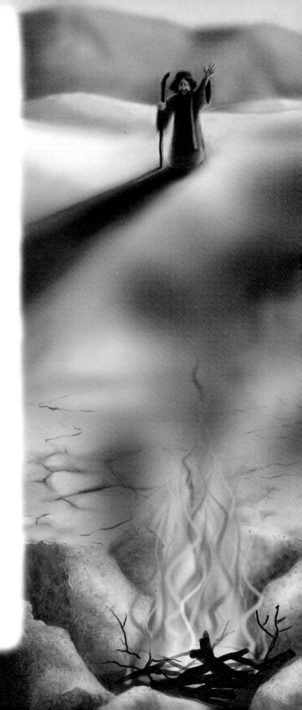

It did not rain.
And Kerith stopped her laughing
song and slowly died.
And God said, "Go."

I walked and ran and walked and ran
a hundred miles or more
through crisp and broken grass
and ground cracked open,
until I came to where God said,
"Stop here.
"My friend the widow and her son
will care for you."
I asked for bread and just a drop
to drink.
She gave the last she had
and thought we all would die.

But God refilled her bowl and jug.
Each day we had enough
to eat and drink.
And no rain came.

One day the boy got sick.
And sick, and sick.
His mother rocked and cried.
I watched and prayed.
He died.

"What have you done?" the mother screamed.
"You and your God?
I gave you drink. I gave you bread.
My son is dead."

I shook my head and sighed.
(Who knows the ways of God?)
I carried him inside and prayed,
"O Lord, my God, have pity on us all."
I laid myself upon the child and cried,
"O Lord, bring life."

He breathed.
Alive!
I carried him to her alive!

She held him close and rocked and sang,
"You speak the truth.
Your Lord is God.
Our friend the Lord is God."

And still it did not rain.
Spring, summer, fall, winter.
Spring, summer, fall, winter.
Spring, summer . . . no rain.
Not a drop.

God said, "It's time to stop.
Stop hiding, Elijah.
Go find King Ahab."

I walked and ran across a land
scraped bare of green.
The sky blazed down like cloudless brass.
Cows moaned for food, and children cried (or died).

"You, Elijah," King Ahab stormed
with finger jabbed.
"You brought this trouble on our land.
You and your silly curse at God's command."

"Not I," I shouted back.
"It's you. You serve the Baals.
You killed true prophets of our God,
You and your wife, Queen Jezebel.

"Bring all your prophets, all those hundreds.
It's time to know whose God is God.
Your God is fake, and ours is REAL!"

We built two altars made of stone.
We piled on wood and meat.
But no one dared to light a fire.

"Stand here, all you people," I shouted.
"How long will you go back and forth
between this Baal and God?
Can Baal light fire?
Can God?"

Baal's prophets shouted by the hundreds,
"O hear us, Baal, come light our fire."
They danced till noon
and shouted till their voices hurt.

I watched and said,
"Perhaps your god is thinking hard,
or maybe he's just busy."

They danced and screamed till afternoon.
Their offering lay as cold as stone.

"I guess your Baal is on a trip."
I laughed. (They were so wrong.)
"Or maybe he's just tired and gone to sleep.
I'm sure he'll answer soon."

By evening all their voice was gone.
They fell exhausted in a heap,
but no fire came.

As darkness settled like a cloak,
I motioned to the people.
"Come here," I softly said.
"You've seen enough to know
what Baal can't do.
Now watch the hand of God."

I placed twelve stones
(one for each tribe),
arranged the wood and meat.
I stood and looked and thought and prayed
and said, "Here's what we need:
twelve pots of water poured on top
and splashing underneath."

The people poured, then sat and watched.
And no one dared to breathe.

I prayed, "My Lord, these people need
to know Your power,
that what I've said is true.
Please show Your strength this holy day
and bring them back to You."

ND FIRE EXPLODED FROM THE SKY
ND LAPPED ALONG THE GROUND!

The Lord is God!" the people cried.
The Lord, the Lord is God!"

"And now, King Ahab," I said,
'I think it's going to rain.
Go get a bite to eat."

I climbed to the top of Mount Carmel
and waited through the night.
The stars were brilliant sparkling jewels
against an inky sky.

My ears were full of thundering rain.
I shook my head and watched the sky.
Clouds?
Not one.

At last the sun came up
and shimmered on a glassy sea,
which mirrored back a brilliant blue of sky.
Clouds?
Not one.
Still my ears were full of thundering rain.
I bowed and prayed.

I sent a servant child to watch.
"Look past the sea," I said.
"Look far away, beyond the edge."
He hurried back.
"Clouds?" I asked.
"Not one," he said.

I prayed.
And torrent rain still thundered
through my head.

"Please look again," I begged.
"Not one," he said—

until the seventh time.
He tiptoed back and whispered small,
"I think I saw a little cloud.
It's far away, no bigger than my hand.
Could that mean anything at all?"

I leaped and yelled, "It's time to go!
Tell Ahab he must jump into his chariot,
or rain will wash him down the mountain!"

The cloud grew huge and filled the sky,
which turned from blue to black,
and lightning streaked from clouds to rocks,
and thunder shook the ground.

King Ahab scrambled to his chariot.
He lashed a whip above his horse
and shouted, "Run!"

Wind came at first in tiny puffs,
then roared
and snapped off trees.
I jammed my cloak into my belt
and ran
ahead of the chariot.
Hail bounced around me.
I ran,
faster than Ahab.
Rain whipped my face.
I ran.
Thunder crashed about my ears.
I ran.
Rain splashed and rushed and splattered
and filled the thirsty land.
I ran and ran—
all the way to Jezreel.

But Ahab was embarrassed,
and so was Queen Jezebel.
God had answered with fire.
God had answered with rain.
Baal had answered with nothing.

I knew I had to hide—again.
Again I ran.
I ran at night and hid by day
and watched for Ahab and his men.
I ran and walked a hundred miles
until I was so tired, so sad, so hurt,
I sat and cried
under a broom tree
that gave me shade.

"Can't I just die?" I said to God.
"I've had enough," I prayed—
and slept.

God's angel came and gave me bread and drink.
I ate and drank and went to sleep.

The angel came again and gave me more.
Again I ate and drank.
The angel said, "Be strong,
You must move on."

And God came near
and said,
"Why are you here?"

"O Lord, my God," I cried,
"I've worked so hard for You.
I've walked and run a thousand miles.
I've prayed down rain and fire.
But all Your people turn away.
They tear Your altars down.
Your prophets all are killed.
I am all that's left."

God said, "Stand out on the mountain.
I will meet you there."

I stood
and waited for my Lord.

A mighty wind roared,
tore the mountain apart,
broke the rocks around me.

But the Lord was not in the wind.

After the wind there was an earthquake.
The mountain shook beneath my feet.
I flattened myself against the ground.
But the Lord was not in the earthquake.

After the earthquake there was a fire.
Flames raced up and down the mountain,
came within inches of my cloak.
But the Lord was not in the fire.

Still I stayed
and waited
for God.

Then came a quiet voice,
and God whispered:
"Elijah, why are you here?"

Again I told my story—
only this time it didn't seem so important.

"You are not finished," said God.
"And you are not alone.

"I've kept seven thousand
people as My own
who have not bowed to Baal.

"You'll have to walk and run again
[four hundred miles this time].
But on your way, you'll find a friend.
Elisha is his name."

I traveled down the slope alone.
My feet were tired and sore.
My cloak was heavy on my back,
as heavy as the work that I had done
and still had left to do.

Elisha burst into my view,
so strong he drove twelve yoke of ox.
I threw my cloak around his neck,
and we went on as two.

Much later, when my work was done,
God said, "It's time to leave
the earth.
Your home is now with Me."

I saw a whirlwind
spinning, spinning, spinning
toward the ground.

Wind whistled, roared, and shrieked,
and from inside sprang out
a blazing chariot with fiery, fiery horses.
And God said, "Come."

I tossed my cloak upon the ground
(Elisha picked it up)
and stepped aboard.

This time I didn't run and run.
I rode a wind to heaven.

"If the Lord is God, follow him."
—I Kings 18:21

Elijah knew that God is real, so he did all that God told him to do. This meant running and walking for hundreds of miles. It meant doing lots of scary things such as going against evil King Ahab and Queen Jezebel. It even meant standing alone against all the prophets of Baal. But Elijah kept on following all that God told him. God used him to show lots of people His power. Elijah lived an exciting life. But even more important, he knew God. And God took care of Elijah, even in the end.